Two Little D
Get Lost

Story by Annette Smith
Illustrations by Lisa Simmons

Dilly Duck said to Dally Duck,
"Let's play in the puddles, today."

The two little ducks
ran down the hill.

A little green frog
jumped out of a puddle.

"Hello," said the little green frog.
"I am looking for a friend.
Will you come and play
in the long grass with me?"

"Yes," said Dilly Duck and Dally Duck.
"We will come with you."

They ran into the long grass
with the little green frog.

The little ducks went fast
but the little green frog went faster.

"Where has the little green frog gone?"
said Dilly Duck. "We can't see him."

“And we can’t see Mother Duck!”
said Dally Duck.
“We are lost!”

“Quack! Quack! Quack!”
said Dilly Duck and Dally Duck.

Mother Duck quacked,
"Little ducks, little ducks,
where are you?"

"We are lost in the long grass,"
they said. "We can't see you."

"Stay where you are,"
quacked Mother Duck.
"I will come and get you."

"Quack! Quack! Quack!"

said the two little ducks.

"We will not go away again,"

said Dilly Duck and Dally Duck.